KAMRYN SAYS GOODBYE TO PAPA

Kamryn Says Goodbye to Papa

By Liza Alvarez

CONTENTS

Dedication vi

- 1

- 2

- 3

- 4

- 5

- 6

- 7

- 8

- 9

- 10

- 11

- 12

- 13

About The Author 14

Celebrating the memory of my Daddy Jose A. Alvarez. There are not enough words to express how much I love and miss you.

I am truly thankful I was able to spend the last year of your life caring for you. I would not have changed it for anything in the world. Although I would give anything to have one more day with you to hear you call me a darn fool or hear you say alright...okay, I know you are no longer suffering.

I remember telling Amy "I was your favorite" even though we knew your favorite was really Kamryn!

I can only pray you left this earth knowing how much I truly love you. Thank you for being the best father and grandfather to us.

You are deeply missed and loved but will never be forgotten!

Love Always

OUR STORY BEGAN THE FIRST TIME YOU HELD ME IN YOUR ARMS.

I KNEW FROM THAT DAY WE WOULD BE BEST FRIENDS AND YOU WOULD NEVER LEAVE ME.

EVERY YEAR WE CELEBRATED MY BIRTHDAY WITH
YOUR FAMOUS STRAWBERRY SHORTCAKE.
YUMMY, HOW MUCH I LIKED TO EAT ALL THE
STRAWBERRIES OFF THE CAKE.

I REMEMBER SITTING NEXT TO YOU EVERY MORNING AND PRETENDING TO BE JUST LIKE YOU. MOM GAVE YOU COFFEE AND I HAD TEA, BUT I DID NOT KNOW THE DIFFERENCE. OH, HOW I LOOKED UP TO YOU PAPA.

WHENEVER I WAS SICK, YOU WOULD SIT ME ON YOUR LAP AND MAKE ME FEEL BETTER. I THOUGHT YOU HAD MAGIC POWERS!

WHEN IT WAS NICE OUTSIDE, YOU WOULD ALWAYS TAKE ME TO THE PARK. OUR FAVORITE THING TO DO WAS SLIDE DOWN TOGETHER ON THE BIG SLIDE.

WHEN I WAS SCARED, YOU WOULD LET ME CLIMB ON YOU AND GRAB YOUR HAIR UNTIL I WAS NOT SCARED ANYMORE.

IN THE SUMMERTIME WE WOULD GO TO THE BEACH TO
BUILD SANDCASTLES. YOU ALWAYS LET ME JUMP ON THE
SANDCASTLES AFTER YOU BUILT THEM.

YOU WOULD PLAY BASKETBALL WITH ME THE SAME WAY
YOU PLAYED WITH MOMMY WHEN SHE WAS MY AGE.

ONCE YOU STARTED TO GET SICK, WE WERE NOT ABLE TO GO OUTSIDE TO DO ALL THE FUN THINGS WE USED TO DO. BUT WE STILL HAD FUN INSIDE READING BOOK AFTER BOOK AFTER BOOK.

I MISSED YOU SO MUCH WHEN YOU WENT INTO THE HOSPITAL. MOM SAID I COULD WEAR YOUR HAT UNTIL YOU CAME BACK HOME. I COULD NOT WAIT TO SEE YOU AGAIN!

I WAITED AND WAITED FOR YOU TO COME HOME, BUT MOMMY SAID THAT YOU WERE SICK, AND YOU COULD NOT LEAVE THE HOSPITAL. ONCE THE DOCTOR SAID IT WAS SAFE FOR VISITORS, MOMMY TOOK ME TO GO SEE YOU. I WAS SO HAPPY TO FINALLY SEE YOU AGAIN!

I KEPT WAITING FOR YOU TO GET BETTER SO YOU COULD COME HOME AND PLAY WITH ME, BUT THAT NEVER HAPPENED. I REMEMBER WHEN I CLIMBED INTO YOUR BED, AND YOU READ ME A BOOK FOR THE LAST TIME. MOMMY SAID YOU WERE TIRED, AND IT WAS TIME FOR YOU TO GO TO SLEEP IN HEAVEN.

IT IS NOW TIME FOR ME TO SAY GOODBYE TO YOU PAPA. I WILL ALWAYS REMEMBER THE TIMES WE SHARED AND THE FUN THINGS WE DID. I WILL ALWAYS LOVE YOU AND HOLD YOU IN MY HEART. YOU WILL FOREVER BE MY BEST FRIEND!

Liza Alvarez is an Author, Social Worker, Ordained Minister, entrepreneur, and proud mother of four amazing children. She decided to write her first children's book after losing her father in February 2021. After finding it difficult to accept the sudden loss of her father, she decided she would turn to writing which resulted in a children's book based on the relationship between her father and her youngest daughter Kamryn. Not only did writing the book allow her a way to grieve, but it also reminded her how fortunate and lucky she was to have a father as amazing as the one she was blessed with. This book was written with love and hope of keeping her father's memory alive while sharing with the world how special he was to so many people.

I would like to thank the people closest to me for the emotional, spiritual and mental support during the last year. To my partner Dashun, and my children Kris, Kayla, Kaitlyn and Kamryn, thank you for stepping in to help when I needed you most and not complaining. I could not have done it without you guys. I know all of our lives changed and at times it was challenging but I will forever appreciate and love you guys for the way you cared for and loved my Daddy.
Thank you to everyone outside of my home that did not forget about me and continues to support me through my good and bad days.